THE YALE DRAMA SERIES

David Charles Horn Foundation

The Yale Drama Series is funded by the generous support of the David Charles Horn Foundation, established in 2003 by Francine Horn to honor the memory of her husband, David. In keeping with David Horn's lifetime commitment to the written word, the David Charles Horn Foundation commemorates his aspirations and achievements by supporting new initiatives in the literary and dramatic arts.

Apologies to Lorraine Hansberry (You Too, August Wilson)

RACHEL LYNETT

Foreword by Paula Vogel

Yale UNIVERSITY PRESS   NEW HAVEN & LONDON

Yale University Press books may be purchased in quantity for educational, business, or promotional use. For information, please e-mail sales.press@yale.edu (U.S. office) or sales@yaleup.co.uk (U.K. office).

Set in ITC Galliard and Sabon types by Integrated Publishing Solutions.
Printed in the United States of America.

ISBN 978-0-300-26146-2 (paperback : alk. paper)
Library of Congress Control Number: 2022931500
A catalogue record for this book is available from the British Library.

This paper meets the requirements of ANSI/NISO Z39.48-1992 (Permanence of Paper).

10 9 8 7 6 5 4 3 2 1

Contents

Foreword

Ⓘt is always a difficult thing to adjudicate. I always have a
pile of plays that tug at my heart, the ones unchosen
and the ever present wish that there were more resources
I could share.

The Yale drama prize was no different from the many
times I have read through stacks of plays, been encouraged
and ebullient at how good the work in those stacks is, but
again, knowing there can only be one prize given. In this
way the Yale prize belies our field: there is no "winning" in
a competition, rather a field of colleagues who, through per-
severance, become a circle of colleagues.

Early in my reading the stack I read the first two pages of
Apologies to Lorraine Hansberry: but not the whole play.

It was a bang of a start to the play; I felt that the play had
grabbed hold of my shirt, and told me, "Listen!" So after
two pages, I thought I should return to the script after I had
read through the entire pile. I have discovered that a play
can (and should) demand that you read it on page one. So
after I read every play in the stack, I returned to the pages
and encountered *Apologies to Lorraine Hansberry (You Too,
August Wilson)* in its entirety in one sitting.

The play is set in a world that cannot possibly exist in

America, as Rachel Lynett tells us: "The place that this play happens in doesn't exist. And will never exist. . . . The play is set in what was once Northern California, now its own state called Bronx Bay. Bronx Bay is all black. Only black people live there and it's black as f* ck. . . . It is the opposite of realism yet it's deeply real. And just because the play is a lie, that doesn't give you an excuse to ignore the truth in it."

There is a boldness and confidence in this writer. Lynett creates a world after the Second Civil War that occurred in 2016–2019 upon Trump's election. And as a result of victories in that war, four new nation-states were created: Bronx Bay, a gated community for Black residents in what used to be Northern California; Tejan for Latinos, located south of Houston; Quint, the nation-state for queers, north of Eugene, Oregon; and Mixi for the nation-state south of Tampa.

And right up front, the play begins with a direct audience address: "Hi. I'm Alice in the play. But right now, I'm basically the playwright, addressing you directly. White folx call what I'm about to do 'exposition.' But the black folx in the audience know I'm about to preach. The world you're about to see ain't yours. It's not a parallel universe, it's not an alternate reality. It's something else. It lives in the imagination of every person of color who has had to live through the Trump administration. . . . To the white people here, thanks for coming, I guess. Your visitor pass to Bronx Bay will expire in 100 minutes and we will keep watch."

From the gitgo, Rachel Lynett lets me as a white audience member know: this play is not about you, white person. I am allowed to watch for 100 minutes as the Black actors and characters examine the tensions that occur when one's identity is declared as a monolithic thing: one's Blackness, in a nation space that is gated to Latine, Asian, indigenous, white, and every other racial identity, becomes the defining criteria to living in Bronx Bay.

We watch as relationships fray upon the entrance of a newcomer, Yael. Yael is Jules's girlfriend, but her entry is questioned by the block when Alice and others discover that Yael's mother lives in Tejan.

What is identity? What is Blackness? When the residents choose their race as the main focus of identity, other facets of the citizens' identities cause ruptures and tensions on the block. The back stories, the grief and losses from the civil war fester; along with the inability to become pregnant in a nation-state that prioritizes families; the fluidity of sexual desire also ignites watching and suspicion.

If the residents of Bronx Bay fence themselves in, are they also fencing in past ideologies of policing from the toxicity they think they can exclude? What happens if the issues that divide a collective—the regulation of child-bearing, the exclusion of those who may center the other end of the hyphen, such as gay-Black, or Mexican-Black—are unexamined when the gates go up? What do we fence in with ourselves when we fence people out?

There is a primary reason that goes unsaid: the desirability to get out of White America. As Ms. Lynett tells us: "People can kill us, torture us, rape us, and nothing happens. Being a separatist is such a sexy fantasy because that way at least people won't kill us for just existing. But if you're one of those people who say 'well what about Black on Black crime,' this play isn't for you. You're not going to get it. Set it down and go read *A Raisin in the Sun* instead."

We will discuss the layers of apologies later.

What occurs in Part 1 is that Alice, a fusion chef who lives with Lorenzo, becomes increasingly discontent that Yael, who has come to join Jules in Bronx Bay, has been let in (there is the unacknowledged irony that Alice's mother is Korean, and hence her food is fusion-inspired).

Underneath the face-value acceptance of sexuality, and the "no big deal" of Jules's desire to live with Yael, is the revelation that Jules had been engaged to Alice's brother who died in the war: in Jules's closet, in the back, hangs the wedding dress.

The end of Part 1 is the dissolution of harmony on the block in Bronx Bay as the residents police their own.

Part 2 opens with an alienation device: we are still in Bronx Bay, we are still in the neighborhood. But now the residents are living in other houses on the block: Jules and Alice are a couple, as are Lorenzo and Izaak. In this world, the focus on the block is creating life and families for the couples. We learn that there are regulations in Bronx Bay that do not let single women over thirty procreate: there is obligatory surgery.

Into this world, Yael enters as a stranger. Why, her neighbors query on their porches, is a single woman who is "getting up there" toward thirty allowed to be inside the gate?

This second act closes in how women, in any revolution, give up their control of their bodies; their reproduction is policed.

The play ends with a remarkable device, which happens when the action and the characters locked in conflict get a text from the playwright. It is a perfect ending in that the ending of these conflicts about race and sexuality and our own bodies can only be resolved by each person on stage for themselves, and each person in the audience for ourselves.

There is no one pathway to becoming a playwright, much less any other theater artist. Rachel Lynett is not an exception to the finding of her voice in America. For the first eighteen years of her life she lived in Los Angeles. She did not know theater; but she knew Disney movies as a girl and loved them. Her mother saved up to bring Rachel to see *The Lion King* at the Center Theatre Group, and she adored the show, but thought that was because, after all, it was Disney.

She went to Notre Dame for her undergraduate studies, and studied classics and anthropology, switching to romance languages for a moment, considered film criticism, and ended up with a double major in gender studies and theater, with Italian as a minor. For one day in her junior year, Rachel needed to fulfill a necessary credit in arts, and walked into a script analysis class. Her professor gave the students plays written by Caryl Churchill, *The Vibrator Play* by Sarah Ruhl: all of the plays were written by women, and none of them were strictly realistic.

She walked out of the class determined to remain in theater.

But her experience shares much in common with other playwrights of color (I remember hearing Jocelyn Bioh talk about a similar hazing in her undergraduate theater department): if she tried out, as she did for *Proof,* she was told that she was the best that had tried out, but the sisters in the play had to be sisters, and she was Black, and no one else from the Black community had tried out and so . . . it always came down to race. In *A Streetcar Named Desire,* she was cast as the flower seller.

Like so many actors who convert to writing for the dearth of in-depth roles, and thereby create richer possibilities for the generation of women behind them, in truth she had started writing in high school. Her annual class shows were written by her, but she told her classmates: "Take the script, do what you want to it, just leave me alone. I am going to become a lawyer."

Her first play that she claims as her own she wrote in her senior year, *Threshold.* Rachel heard scenes from her play, while designing the lights for her own production.

In order to take a gamble with an uncertain path to theater, it is necessary to feel the uplift of watching others embody your words. To resonate with joy at the experience. Rachel Lynett couldn't deny what she felt when her words were embodied by collaborators.

And so when a professional artistic director came to campus, Rachel pleaded for a stage management internship. The woman said yes: you are going to be in—Arkansas!

"Arka—Um, Where are you?" Her mentor suggested during Rachel's internship that she take a playwriting workshop. In the workshop, her faculty suggested that she apply for the MFA in playwriting. She was already there: why not? In Walmart Country.

She loved it: and took graduate English courses, and wrote a lot of plays. The only production she would receive in the program was her thesis play.

And so she started her own company to produce plays in grad school: she had strict rules about not producing her own work. She produced twenty writers in ten-minute festivals. She produced two full-lengths, and a residency in a children's shelter. Because grad school said, "You do not get to be produced until your thesis," Rachel determined to do it herself.

As Rachel recounts her history, I am struck by her curiosity, her ambition not to be contained by rules or specialization. She was equipping herself with everything she would need. The Open Fence Coalition was the name of her first theater: she didn't believe in the exclusion of fences, and hence, in her theater, her fence was open, invitational, inclusive. And of course, Rachel nodded to one of her theatrical ancestors, August Wilson and his remarkable *Fences*.

"Neighbors keep fences to keep people out. There is no way to get into theater. But theater for everybody."

While in graduate school, Rachel Lynett wrote quickly and she read deeply: the words of José Rivera, Caryl Churchill, Young Jean Lee, and Suzan-Lori Parks were inspirational, as were the works of Lorraine Hansberry and August Wilson.

She did not gravitate toward the well-made play.

For other inspiration, Rachel did gravitate toward a local museum and attended two talks about the Black experience in art. Both the white and Black curators, Rachel felt, were monolithic about their depiction of Black identity. Rachel felt provoked by their narrow definitions, and went home and wrote *Apologies to Lorraine Hansberry (You Too, August Wilson)*. She wrote the play in a day.

Rachel Lynett didn't know where it was going, this play.

"I just knew I wanted to break all the rules that I had learned."
She knew her adviser would say, "The playwright's hand is
showing too much; these are your words, not the characters'." It was that narrow.

On the first page of her play, she knew, yes, this is the
playwright's voice. She wrote it in a fever dream. She got to
the end, and she still didn't know where it was going, or
how to end it. But listening to her own play Rachel had a
revelation: that is because it isn't up to me to end it. And on
stage, in performance, the actors get a text from the playwright because: "Theater should be collaborative, and we
playwrights should explore ways to make theater collaborative too."

In October 2019 she wrote the play; in January 2020 she
left Arkansas and her marriage, went to Madison, and started
a whole new life. She wasn't thinking about *Apologies,* she
was thinking about finding an apartment, and starting a new
life.

Rachel did not send the play out; she put it on New Play
Exchange, and she sent it to Yale. And she sent it to Orlando Shakespeare, which will be producing the play in Sep-
tember of 2022.

Not a bad outcome for three submissions.

Rachel Lynett refutes the possibility of ending the play in
violence and pain for her characters; her second act shows the
impossibility that identity be static. "The play is about the
struggle to define identity. It's not being Black in America
viewed through a white lens. What does Black mean through
a Black lens?"

I asked her: "In terms of not containing the play on the
stage, the breaking of the fourth wall, a non-continuity in
action between act 1 and act 2, and having the play end with
the actors resolving the identity dilemma for themselves: are
your other plays like this one?"

Rachel answered that her dramaturg would say her other

plays were leading up to *Apologies:* her resolutions of her plays are strong, "trippy," a shift into another world or reality. Her last scenes change the rules of the play.

I perceive the layers navigating and negotiating a white American theater to talk to Black audience members, actively creating a brown and Black community within a white audience. "How," I asked, "do you define identity?"

"I don't know and that's why I wrote this play. Identity is personal and sociological: the identity which is personal and belongs to us, and the identity which is assigned to us: the sociological. Those of us who don't like the sociological identity assigned to us are constantly struggling whereas other people think, 'the personality assigned to me is exactly the one I want,' living the best life, where for the rest of us, it's a constant battle. 'I want to be THIS, but society tells me I'm *this,* so I can try for a little bit of THIS but for my safety I have to be a little bit of *this . . .*"

If we take fluidity as the organizing principle of *Apologies,* then Rachel Lynett is also playing with our roles as audience members. "White people call this exposition, Black people know this is preach."

The structure, the direct audience address, the unreliability of any narrator, and the way Lynett changes the roles that have been assigned to the cast between the first and second acts: all of this is to shake the ground on which we stand. And yet Lynett eschews theater of cruelty: "Theater should disrupt, challenge, but not be abrasive. Theater of cruelty doesn't compel you to change. But it should be like a playground: it should welcome you. Yes there are bullies on the playground, but you fight back. I like the audience to be a part of it, and that is why it's a playground. First we're gonna laugh, and then we're gonna talk."

So, I asked Rachel Lynett: why and what are the apologies?

"In February theaters always mount the two same plays: *Raisin in the Sun* and *Fences.* And so apologies to Lorraine

Hansberry and August Wilson for having to carry the burden of Black theater. So apologies you had to carry the load of Black representation, because I am about to blow it up." I think of course, of the revolution of Hansberry in the 1950s creating a world in which her characters dare to integrate a white neighborhood: seventy years later Rachel Lynett will dare to write a play that dares to segregate the Bronx Bay. (And I think as well about apologies to Ms. Hansberry because she struggled with the complexity of her gender at a time that it wasn't possible to express it.)

Apologies to August Wilson? I ask her.

"I read *The Ground on Which I Stand* every year, and yes I am against color-blind casting . . . and yes we can build our own theaters, but it is still white people attending it. I don't want to traumatize the Black people while I am talking to the white people. I understand you are here, white people, and you get to eavesdrop this conversation I am having with Black people." Where August Wilson fails a bit, for Rachel Lynett, is that "some of us are multi-racial: I am black, but I am also Latina, Latinx, I can't separate that. I can be more than one thing, why can't you let me be more than one thing? Which is why the divide of August Wilson fails a little bit."

And yet, of course, Rachel Lynett's theatrical revolution can only stand on the ground these two writers stood.

As I read and re-read *Apologies,* there is a lot we do not know in 2022: Are we indeed on the brink of Civil War? Will America finally move toward a more perfect union and stop depleting its politics, its arts, its commerce, from the cultural richness of the majority of its population: people of color? Will we reform ourselves from within in order to reform the outside: the lack of autonomy over our bodies, the police that will kill a Black man selling a single cigarette (and fill in the obscene list of murders of Black citizens at the hands of police); the inequity gap between white lives and the rest of the population?

But I have a feeling that stopped me in my tracks on the second page of Rachel Lynett's *Apologies to Lorraine Hansberry (You Too, August Wilson):* this is a writer who must be read and produced. Rachel Lynett will become the ground on which future writers stand.

Paula Vogel

Production History

*A*pologies to Lorraine Hansberry (*You Too, August Wilson*) received its first professional reading with Mirrorbox Theatre in June 2020.

The play received a professional reading as part of PlayFest 2020 at Orlando Shakes Theatre.

It was developed as part of the Martha Heasley Cox Virgin Play Festival at Magic Theatre in San Francisco in January 2021.
Sonia Fernandez, Interim Artistic Director
Kevin Nelson, Managing Director

The play received its world premiere at Fonseca Theatre in August 2021.

Apologies to Lorraine Hansberry
(You Too, August Wilson)

THE BLOCK
[3w, 2m]

JULES,* she/her/hers, 30s, Black, works at the community
garden

LORENZO,* he/him/his, Black, 30s, works as a game
developer

ALICE,* she/her/hers, 30s, chef, Black, Lorenzo's wife in
Part 1 and Jules's wife in Part 2

YAEL,* she/her/hers, Afro-Latinx, Jules's girlfriend in Part
1, 30s, teacher

IZAAK, he/him/his, Black, artist, 30s, lives on the block,
mostly Lorenzo's friend in Part 1 and Lorenzo's
boyfriend in Part 2

*There is absolutely no reason Jules, Yael, or Lorenzo can-
not be played by a trans actor.

Settings
The place that this play happens in doesn't exist. And will
never exist (see production notes). The play is set in what
was once Northern California, now its own state called Bronx
Bay. Bronx Bay is all black. Only black people live there and
it's black as f* ck. In all set design choices please keep this in
mind.
    The action of the play happens mostly on the block in

front of Jules's, Alice and Lorenzo's, and Izaak's houses on
their front porches and in their lawns. The year is 2020. But
again, a different, impossible 2020.

In Part 1, Bronx Bay is a new state. In Part 2, Bronx Bay
is a gated neighborhood.

Production Notes
This play is a lie. It's not afro-futurism. It's not historically accurate. This play is actually so historically inaccurate,
it's historical heresy. It will never happen, can never happen, and some people would argue should never happen. It
is the opposite of realism yet it's deeply real. And just because the play is a lie, that doesn't give you an excuse to
ignore the truth in it.

Moment Versus Shift
I have a hard time with the word "beat." For me, a moment is a break in the dialogue, a chance for the characters
to reassess. A shift is just a sharp turn in dialogue or action.
It's not necessarily a pause. A moment is a passive action/
pause whereas a shift is an active one.

Playwright's Note
There have been many mornings when I have woken up
and told my partner (who is usually white), "I don't want to
see or talk to any white people today." It's not that I hate
white people. It's that existing in the United States as a
queer person of color is exhausting. And sometimes code-
switching and having to be double, sometime triple con-
scious wears you down. Because of this, sometimes I do
wonder what an all-Black space would look like. But the
irony isn't lost on me that if I went to live in a truly all-Black
city, my partner wouldn't be able to come. Some of my family members (who are Latine) wouldn't be able to come.

Black people aren't safe in the United States. People can
break into our homes and kill us and then only get charged

for shooting at walls, not us. People can kidnap us and no one asks what happened to us. People who kill us over running stop signs, over legally owning a weapon, over selling cigarettes. People can kill us, torture us, rape us, and nothing happens. Being a separatist is such a sexy fantasy because that way at least people won't kill us just for existing.

But if you're one of those people who say "well what about Black on Black crime," this play isn't for you. You're not going to get it. Set it down and go read *A Raisin in the Sun* instead.

Part 1

Prologue

ALICE steps out to address the audience. Designers can have as much or as little fun with this moment as they want. Maybe there are projections of what she's describing? Maybe the set is still being moved on. It should be clear that this isn't quite the beginning of the play but it's also still very much a part of the play.

ALICE   Hi. I'm Alice in the play. But right now, I'm basically the playwright, addressing you directly. White folx call what I'm about to do "exposition." But the black folx in the audience know I'm about to preach. The world you're about to see ain't yours. It's not a parallel universe, it's not an alternate reality. It's something else. It lives in the imagination of every person of color who has had to live through the Trump administration.

So, in this world, after Trump was elected, there was what was known as The Second Civil War. It lasted from November 2016 to August 2019. The war broke out literally after it was announced that the motherfucking electoral college thought it was cool to put a white supremacist with dementia in office. On August 19, 2019, a peace treaty was signed. The compromise was that Trump would stay president but Cory Booker became the new VP. I'm not sure why it had to be him. I think he gave an impassioned speech at the right time. I ain't know. I always knew he was trifflin but I don't really trust Kamala either. So anyway, as part of the "Race War Treaty" four new states were created: Bronx Bay, Tejan, Quint, and Mixi.

7

Technically, the Treaty really only created Mixi, which is everything south of Tampa in Florida. To live in Mixi, you gotta be POC. And that was all good until everyone remembered anti-blackness is international and subconscious, so black people took the Bay. We said, "If it's north of Santa Cruz, it's ours now." And since it was about to be another Civil War, Congress ratified it as a new state. And called it Bronx Bay. Why Bronx Bay? Racism. We wanted it to be called #yayarea but only the real ones know about that. Well, then Latinos were like "Um the fuck?" So everything south of Houston became Tejan. And you gotta be Latine to live there. Then queer people were like "EXCUSE ME," so then everything north of Eugene, Oregon, became Quint. And you gotta be queer to live there. It all gets super intense and I'm sure other groups will protest and be like, What about us. But this, this right here, isn't about them. This right here is about Bronx Bay. To my people, feel free to stomp, whistle, clap, holler. Just know I wanna be outta here in 90 minutes so, you know, do it in a way that don't mess us up while we're on stage. To the white people here, thanks for coming, I guess. Your visitor pass to Bronx Bay will expire in 100 minutes and we will keep watch.

Aight. Let's go.

ALICE starts to leave the stage. The lights change. And then she comes back.

ALICE   Wait. One more thing. In the prologue of *Romeo and Juliet*, Shakespeare tells you everything that's gonna happen in the play, and that's one of the most produced plays in the country. So if anyone's butt hurt about all this exposition, think about the reasons why you're coming for this play but at the same time saying Shakespeare was the greatest playwright of all time.

Aight. For real. I gotta finish putting my makeup on. I'm out.

ALICE *leaves the stage. Lights change.*

Scene 1

JULES *comes out on her front porch, drinking iced tea and reading the newspaper. On stage, we see the front of Jules's, Alice and Lorenzo's, and Izaak's brownstones. In spite of being brownstones, they all have front porches with furniture on the porches unique to each of them. They also all have pristine front lawns.*
    LORENZO *comes out, holding up a copy of* My Bondage and My Freedom *by Frederick Douglass.*

JULES   Why you trying to stunt, Lorenzo?

LORENZO   What?

JULES   Frederick Douglass? You got Audre Lorde hidden in your pants?

LORENZO   You think she'd fit?

JULES   You know you ain't never read *My Bondage and My Freedom.*

LORENZO   What? You got X-ray vision? How can you even see all the way over here?

JULES   I ain't blind. You holdin' it up like you want the whole world to see.

LORENZO   Aight. You right. Alice is reading it. I thought I might —

I don't know. I tried to read it and I was like damn this
is not the light read I was expecting.

JULES   What part of "bondage" seems light to you?

LORENZO   I mean, depending on what you're into—

JULES   Lorenzo!

LORENZO   He was our 16th president. He's why people
that look like you and look like me ain't gotta pick cotton
anymore. I expected this to be, I don't know, at least uplifting. It's depressing as hell.

JULES   It's about slavery! Slavery was depressing.

LORENZO   I mean I guess.
      Yael get in okay?

JULES   Yeah. She got in late last night.

LORENZO   I'm supposed to invite you both to dinner.

JULES   Is this the invitation?

LORENZO   I don't know. I hate having people over.
Alice gets all intense about the kitchen. Thinks she gotta
show off.

JULES   I was actually just about to read the review of her
new restaurant.

LORENZO   Don't. And don't even mention it to her if
you see her.

JULES   Why . . . not?

LORENZO   It was reviewed by Kanome Wyatt. Who is like best friends with Christina Washington and apparently Kanome was completely unfair and misunderstood what she was trying to do.

JULES   I don't know who anyone you just mentioned is.

LORENZO   Well, Kanome is a food critic. But she's very like "power to the people."

JULES   O-kay. Why is that a— [problem]

LORENZO   Alice is making fusion food. Which is not, according to Kanome, you know, power to the people.

JULES   Alice's grandfather was Korean so it makes sense that—

LORENZO   Right. To us, it makes sense. But come on.

LORENZO makes sure ALICE isn't in ear shot.

LORENZO   (*whispering*)
    Soon du gumbo don't sound weird to you?

JULES   Soon to what?

LORENZO   It's a blend of soon du boo, a Korean tofu soup, and gumbo. You know what ain't got no place in gumbo? Tofu.

Shift.

JULES   Are you still inviting me to dinner?

LORENZO   You still wanna come?

JULES   Sure.

LORENZO   I'll ask Alice to make her soon du gumbo.

JULES   No thank you.

LORENZO   See! I knew I wasn't the only

ALICE comes out. She eyes LORENZO. She might have heard more than he thought.

ALICE   Hi Jules.

JULES   Alice.

ALICE   You coming over tonight?

JULES   I just got invited. What time?

ALICE   *(to LORENZO)*
You didn't text her last night?

LORENZO   No. I forgot.

ALICE   I told you to do it while your phone was in your hand.

LORENZO   Yes dear. I realize that. But I didn't so How can we move forward?

ALICE   Don't try that therapist shit on me

LORENZO   I'm not —
We went to couples' therapy in order to—

ALICE   And you ain't gotta air our business either.

JULES   What time for dinner?

ALICE   Seven. You're bringing Yael, right?

JULES nods.

ALICE   I can't believe she was able to come in. I mean, I know a ton of black people who can't get in yet.

JULES   Well, she's moving in with me so housing isn't an issue for her.

LORENZO   Are you excited? It's a big step.

JULES   After watching you two, I'm a little concerned.

ALICE   She's playin'.
       Alright. I gotta go check on the restaurant. Don't talk bad about my food, Lorenzo.

ALICE leaves.

JULES   Your wife is so sweet.

LORENZO   I didn't marry her because she was sweet.

JULES   I feel like this is going to take a turn so I'd like to remind you, Renzo, that just because I like women, that doesn't mean I wanna shoot the shit about how hot your wife is.

LORENZO   She is, though.

JULES   Okay.

Moment.

LORENZO   Yael's Black, right?

JULES   What? Yes. Of course.

LORENZO   Okay, I just —
I never met a Black Yael before.

JULES   Lorenzo. Your name is Lorenzo.

LORENZO   Fair. Alright. See you tonight.

*LORENZO heads inside his house. JULES opens the newspaper
and tries to read it. Then she closes it. And heads inside.*

Scene 2

*Later that evening, on ALICE and LORENZO's porch. YAEL
comes out, holding a glass of wine. She looks around the street,
almost as though she can feel it looking back at her.
    JULES, also holding a glass of wine, comes outside.*

JULES   Hey.

YAEL   Hey.

JULES   Alice can be a bit intense.

YAEL   Yes. That is an understatement.
We're having a second dinner later, right? With meat in it?

JULES nods.

YAEL   Not that it wasn't delicious. I just—

JULES   I get it. I'm always hungry again in like an hour
if I eat only vegetarian dishes.

LORENZO, holding a beer, and ALICE, drinking water, come outside.

ALICE   That's because you overeat.

JULES   I don't—

ALICE   You're just not aware of it. It's in your head. You're not hungry. You're just a being a brat.

JULES   Or I'm hungry. I think I'm old enough to know when I'm hungry.

ALICE   You're not. Most times you're just thirsty.

YAEL   Thank you for a wonderful evening, Alice. It's gorgeous out tonight.

ALICE   Of course. Come over any time.

LORENZO   But knock a couple of times. If we're in the back, we can't hear you.

YAEL   I'm honestly surprised there are brownstones here. Like don't get me wrong. I love them. They're beautiful but why not have a house?

ALICE   We didn't want that much space. After Bronx Bay was established last year, anyone who got in could choose between a house, an apartment, or a brownstone. For some people owning land is a major thing and a lot of land.

LORENZO   Rightfully so.

ALICE   And for some people, I just don't need that much space, you know. If you go further up north, you'll see bigger houses. But the whole state didn't need to be reclaiming plantations.

Moment. YAEL'*s phone rings. She answers*

YAEL   Hola mami. Entre bien.

YAEL *walks away farther down the block (and off stage) to finish the phone call.* ALICE *eyes* JULES.

JULES   Okay, hold on. I speak French. Am I suddenly not Black?

ALICE   You took French in school.

JULES   My mom was Honduran.

ALICE   The mom you don't talk to?

JULES   We don't know enough about—

ALICE   Jules, come on. Her name is Yael, she talks to her mom in Spanish.

JULES   My dad and I sometimes to spoke to each other in Spanish.

ALICE   Your dad is dead, Jules.

LORENZO   Alice! You know her dad died just last year.

ALICE   So did my brother. A lot of people died to protect—

JULES   He didn't die last year. He died right at the beginning of the war. And it's not fair for you to—

ALICE   My uncle died last year. So did Lorenzo's dad. We lost a lot of people, so that makes it even more important to me that we adhere to the rules.

JULES   Alice, you're not —
    Yael is Black. How else would she have gotten in?

ALICE   The system isn't perfect yet. Sometimes the tests take too long to process and—

LORENZO   No offense, Jules. But have you . . . asked?

JULES   Do you ask every Black person you see if they're really Black or not?

ALICE   If they were speaking Spanish, I would.

YAEL returns and notices everyone watching her.

YAEL   Hi. Sorry. My mom was worried that I hadn't called to check in yet.

ALICE   Are you Black?

YAEL   What?

ALICE   Are you Black or not?

Moment.

JULES   This is ridiculous. Alice, you cannot ask—

ALICE   How come you speak Spanish?

YAEL   Why do you cook Korean fusion food?

ALICE   Because my mother was half-Korean.

YAEL   Does that make you not Black?

ALICE   No, it doesn't. Answer my question.

LORENZO   Alice.

ALICE   You realize Bronx Bay is an all-Black state right?
And there are tons of reasons why. Should I list them?

YAEL   Can we go?

JULES   Yeah.
    Um, thanks for dinner for Alice.

LORENZO   No, don't — Let's not end the night this way.
    Yael obviously had to take the DNA test to live here so
it's a moot point.

ALICE   And we've seen how even the DNA test isn't
always foolproof.

YAEL   I'm going home.

YAEL *leaves the front porch and goes next door.*
Moment.

ALICE   If this is the part where I say I'm sorry —

JULES   I didn't ask, but it's more than just a DNA test,
Alice. Yes, sometimes it's faulty but there's a series of tests
you have to pass to get in.

ALICE   None of those tests are perfect. Just last week—

JULES   I can't do this with you tonight, Alice. I'm going
home.

ALICE   She needs to leave, Jules!

JULES   She's Black, Alice!

JULES leaves. LORENZO glares at ALICE.

Scene 3

In an ideal situation, the set rotates so we can see the living rooms of ALICE/LORENZO and JULES/YAEL. All four characters are on stage.

In ALICE/LORENZO's house, LORENZO is watching TV while working on his computer while ALICE is on the couch reading the newspaper.

In JULES/YAEL's living room, JULES is working on her computer and YAEL is on the floor preparing a lesson plan.

In both living rooms it's tense.

LORENZO   I just think you could've been kinder about it. I speak Spanish. You're not hounding me about why I speak Spanish.

YAEL   I just wish you had defended me more.

ALICE   I asked your mother where she was born when I met her.

LORENZO   Which was racist.

JULES   I know, I'm sorry.

ALICE   It wasn't racist. Black people are born all over the world. But you know what else is born all over the world? Anti-blackness.

JULES   It took me by surprise. I just didn't —

Alice is a steamroller, you know, and it took me a second to catch up to what she was —
There are a lot of good reasons why Bronx Bay needs to be all-Black. It's just one state.
Not all the Black people in the country live here but—

YAEL   I understand the reasons why this state needs to exist. I don't need a history lesson.

LORENZO   Yael is obviously not anti-black.

ALICE   I'm sorry. How is that obvious? Because she's with Jules? Jules is borderline anti-black.

LORENZO   Alice —

ALICE   She still uses chemicals in her hair but claims to be natural.

LORENZO   Oh my God. I can't do this with you again.

JULES   You're right. I shouldn't've —
   I'm glad you're here.

YAEL   Yeah.

JULES   I mean it. I am. Thank you for moving here.

YAEL   You don't think it's kind of strange there are entire states you can't go to?

JULES   What?

YAEL   It doesn't bother you that you can't go to Tejan. Just to visit?

JULES   No. Because I understand what it is and why it
needs to be this way. It was the only to end the War.

ALICE   Why is everyone treating me like some kind of
Disney villain?
   I'm just reminding everyone that there are rules. People
died for those rules. And to recklessly abandon them—

LORENZO   No one is abandoning them. Yael took the
DNA test. Like we all did.

ALICE   Did she? Plus they're sloppy with delivery and
enforcement. I took the test, I was 75% Black so I didn't
have to take the other tests. Meanwhile didn't you have to
do the electric slide or something?
   What exactly are all of the tests? Why isn't that public
knowledge?

LORENZO   Alice, you need to — We should apologize.

ALICE   I'm not apologizing until she tells me she's
Black. Definitively.

LORENZO   What? Are you going to ask the governor to
see what tests she took?

ALICE   Oh! That's a good idea. I bet I could at least
request her DNA test.

LORENZO   Alice.

ALICE *pulls out her phone to start researching.*

YAEL   My mom lives in Tejan.

JULES   Oh.

YAEL   So like, long term, how do you meet my mother?
You can't go to Tejan and she can't come here.

JULES *isn't sure what to say.*

ALICE *(reading)*
    The only way to request a DNA test if you're related.
And usually it's as a defense in court.
    Jules and I are kind of related.

LORENZO   Legally. Kind of. But that's not the related
they're talking about.

ALICE   Legal relation should count.

LORENZO   Alice.

ALICE   I called her mom Aunty.

LORENZO   We're Black. If you don't call adults Uncle
or Aunty, we don't fuck with them.

ALICE   Yes. We are Black. Yael though? Something in
the chicken grease don't smell right.

LORENZO   Alice, please let this go.

ALICE *keeps researching on her phone.*

JULES   So. If your mom lives in Tejan, um —
    Are you parents together? Where does your dad live?

YAEL   Jules.

JULES   I just assumed that —
    We met in New York. And I always went to visit you in
Jersey. I didn't even think to —

I realize I never —
I mean, it feels like a weird thing to ask someone. But —
But life is gonna hella weird if I don't. So, are you not
Black?

YAEL   I'm Dominican.

JULES   O-kay. Um —

YAEL   But I'm also Black. You can be both.

JULES   I think a lot of Dominicans would disagree with
you.

YAEL   And you and I would disagree with them.

JULES   So your mom doesn't see herself as Black?

YAEL   I'm not my mom.

JULES   O-kay. Well what about your dad?

YAEL   I'm not talking about this with you.

ALICE   Oh! That's right. You can request a proof copy
as long as you list "reasonable doubt" and are able to
explain your doubt in front of a jury.

LORENZO   Alice.

ALICE   It's like a $50 mailing fee. I bet Jules could just
ask for Yael's. Shouldn't Yael have a copy?

LORENZO   Alice.

ALICE   Don't Alice me. I'm just—

Before ALICE *can finish talking, she kneels over, gagging physically.*

ALICE   Be right back.

She runs out of the room. LORENZO *looks after her but doesn't get up.*

JULES   I'm sorry —

YAEL   Thank you

JULES   But I need to know.

YAEL *stops working.*

YAEL   My dad was Haitian. But I never met him. Are we done with this now?

JULES   But you identify as Black. Right?

YAEL   I've already said that I—
    If I told you to choose to between being Black and being gay, which would you choose?

JULES   I'm both.

YAEL   Right. But don't places like Bronx Bay and Tejan and Quint kind of force you to choose?

JULES   No, I don't —
    I'm proudly out. But I would only ever live in Bronx Bay.

ALICE *comes back.*

LORENZO   You okay?

ALICE   Yeah. It's just the baby.

LORENZO   Should I call Doctor Reynolds?

ALICE   No. I'm alright.

A moment.

ALICE   I actually might go lay down for a bit.

LORENZO   Okay. You know stress only makes it worse?

ALICE   I'm not stressed. I just want — I want us to be safe.

ALICE *kisses him and then leaves the room.*

YAEL   It feels like a broken system.

JULES   Why did you move here if you didn't—

YAEL   Because I want to be with you. And you will only live here.

JULES   This is the safest place for me.

YAEL   Is it? We're talking a lot about anti-blackness but what about queer-phobia in the black community? Isn't Quint technically safer?

JULES   Yael. I don't —
   Let's not do this tonight.

YAEL   Fine. I'm going to bed. I'm tired anyway.

YAEL leaves. Moment. LORENZO picks up his phone to call
JULES. He keeps the phone on speaker. She holds it to her ear.
We can see and hear both of them.

LORENZO   Hi.

JULES   Hi

LORENZO   Is it as rough over there as it is over here?

JULES   Yes. Probably.

LORENZO   Alice is about to ask you for Yael's DNA
test.

JULES   DNA test won't help much. I'm sure she tested
as Black but —

LORENZO   But?

JULES   I uh —
    It's been a long night. I'm tired. Goodnight, Renzo.

JULES hangs up. And looks out into the audience.

Scene 4

Lights change with house lights at half.
    ALICE comes back out, dressed up a professor. She has a
dry-erase board and a marker as if she's preparing a lecture.
(It's up to the director and the actor what she writes on the
board, but a note here should be that it is completely in con-
trast with what she's saying. As she talks about black trauma,
what she writes should focus on Black joy. As if joy is fighting
its way forward.)

ALICE   I have already made it clear that I am a chef. So
this is obviously one of those highly theatrical moments
where a character steps out of the world to relay some
information to you. And if that wasn't obvious, luckily, I
have stated it plainly. So we're all on the same page. Why
do it this way and not neatly tuck into the world of play,
maybe some highly tense moment of dialogue? Well, because y'all don't listen. Y'all like to pretend like you missed
it. So here I am in a tweed jacket, giving you more exposition. I know it's exposition, you know it's exposition. But
here we are. I believe in your programs there's a blank
page where you can take notes. It is not my fault if you did
not think to bring a pencil to a play. How were you gonna
take notes in your programs? How were you gonna get my
autograph.

Ready? So our histories are similar, in the beginning.
Christopher Columbus still sailed the ocean blue, although
it's important to me that y'all know he never actually
stepped a foot in the United States so I don't know why
we're obsessed with including him in our history books
but leave out—oh I don't know—the Chinese Exclusion
Act of 1882 which totally happened in the United States.

Anyway, so slavery still happened. Thanks for that. No
I haven't forgotten or forgiven. But here's where it gets
tricky. Abraham Lincoln ran against Frederick Douglass,
who was pretending to be a white man. Frederick Douglass won and became the 16th president of the United
States. He wrote it into law that all slaves were freed. Point
blank. And should be paid for their labor.

Well, as you can imagine, lotta people didn't like that.
So, the Civil War happened. The North won. And the
slaves were freed and given 40 acres and a mule.

Well, sorta. Frederick Douglass wrote a law that said all
slaves were entitled to 40 acres and a mule but Congress
pushed back because there wasn't "enough" land. So then
it was each family got 40 acres and a mule and family was

loosely defined. Like if you're fifth cousin, twice removed, got land, you ain't getting no land. And we all know how trifflin cousins can be. So what happened was an elite class of land-owning Black folk hired the "lower class" of Black folk to work for them. For pennies. Frederick Douglass didn't like it but didn't matter because he was shot during one of his speeches. And his security did nothing about it because days before, people discovered he was Black. It was an open secret. But some people are slow. After that, white people went wild. I mean, let's be real. White people always doin' wild shit but this was one of those peak moments. They burned down the land that was given to the elite Black landowners and made it so nothing could grow on that land again. They said they'd rather destroy the soil than let a nigger have it.

ALICE *wheels off her white erase board.*

Scene 5

The next evening. LORENZO *and* JULES *are rolling a blunt on* IZAAK's *front porch.*

IZAAK   Where's Alice tonight?

LORENZO   Work.

IZAAK   Didn't you tell her you quit smoking?

LORENZO   No. She asked me to quit and I said "I hear you." I cannot be held accountable if she misunderstood my intention.

IZAAK   Right.

JULES *finishes rolling and smokes it first. It's a deep inhale.*

IZAAK   Okay, calm down. We're sharing, remember?

JULES   Sorry.

She passes the blunt to IZAAK.

IZAAK   What's going on with you? Didn't your girl move in? Shouldn't you be—

JULES   I don't want to talk about it.

IZAAK   This is why I stay single. Y'all be trippin.

LORENZO   You stay single 'cause don't nobody got time for that artist temperament of yours.

JULES   Oh, is that what we're calling it now?

LORENZO   Feels rude to say he be throwing tantrums.

IZAAK   I do not throw tantrums. I'm a grown-ass man.

JULES   What happened to Dom?

IZAAK   He said he wanted more commitment than I was able to give him.

JULES   Uh huh.

IZAAK   Y'all coming to my art opening next weekend?

JULES   I don't know.

LORENZO   Your work is . . . um . . . depressing.

IZAAK   I'm sorry recording our history through artistic expression is depressing for you.

LORENZO   Thank you. I appreciate the apology.
Remember that one show back in New York where it
was all about barb wire and lynching?

JULES   Oh my God, yes. The show that was supposed to
uplifting.

IZAAK   It wasn't about lynching. It was about the ma-
terial used to —
Whatever. That's the show that got me on MacArthur
shortlist.

JULES   If it hadn't been for the war, you would've got it.

IZAAK   Thanks.

Moment.

JULES   What's the show about?

IZAAK   I did a photography series on black kids going
to school for the first time in Bronx Bay. Like, I photo-
graphed the same kids for a week. You shoulda seen how
their faces lit up. It was like . . . I don't know what it was
like . . . inspiring. For the first time, these kids won't be
ignored, they won't be told they're not smart enough,
they won't —
I mean, fuck.
It's just —
Y'all should come.

JULES   It's Saturday?

IZAAK   Next Saturday is the opening, yeah. But it'll be
up all month.

LORENZO   Maybe I'll talk Alice into going.

Moment.

JULES   So not all black people live in Bronx Bay. Like obviously some people chose not to live here.

LORENZO   Jules. This isn't— [the time]

JULES   Wait. I swear I'm going somewhere.

LORENZO   I just don't—

JULES   So, like there were black people, there are black people who actively support and protect white supremacy.

IZAAK   Yeah. Duh. That's why we had to take the tests.

JULES   But, okay. So if all skinfolk aren't kinfolk, then isn't fair to reason that some kinfolk aren't skinfolk?

LORENZO   Jules, this isn't—

IZAAK   So non-Black people. Who are just what? Down with us?

JULES   . . . yea. Is that so hard to believe? And isn't going by percentages the exact same thing white people did us? And yea there's the implicit bias test but that's not foolproof either. Some of our biases were inherited and socialized into us so —
   Like we've basically re-invented the brown paper bag test and put it in reverse.

LORENZO   You took an implicit bias test?

JULES   You didn't?

Moment.

IZAAK   Jules, what's going on?

JULES   I'm just —
Alice's grandfather was Korean. Lorenzo, your mom is
Mexican.

LORENZO   My mom is Afro-Mexican and she had to
flee Mexico because her people, my people, were being
slaughtered.

JULES   Right. I know. I —
Okay. My mom was born in Honduras but my mom's
mom was British. Am I not Black enough? What does
"Black" mean anyway? Does Black mean African? Does it
mean anyone with dark skin? And I know this had to be
our reality. That this is just one small space but what if
someone else needed shelter? And wanted to be in community with the community they perceived to be theirs?

Moment.

IZAAK   Last week, two different families got evicted. Had
to leave the state. One of them was just a white woman
who dreadlocked her hair and tanned herself.
She taught African Diasporic History at the college. And
no one could believe she wasn't Black. So people like her?
You're saying people who try on our culture like a Hal-
loween costume should be able to stay?

JULES   No, I —
Obviously not people like her but people who are I
don't know what I'm saying.

LORENZO   She's just high.

JULES   Yeah.
I should head home. See you later.

JULES leaves. Moment.

IZAAK   Anything you want to tell me?

LORENZO   Nah.

IZAAK   How's the game you're working on?

LORENZO   It's great. I think they're really gonna like it.

IZAAK   If you tell me what's going on, it'll make it easier for everyone. I know you remember how things went for you when you weren't honest before. I don't want to have to—

LORENZO   I ain't got shit to say.

LORENZO gets up and leaves. It's tense. Too tense.

Scene 6

Later that evening. JULES is on her front porch, drinking a beer. ALICE, in her chef uniform, comes walking down the block, heading home. They see each other. Without anyone saying anything at all, ALICE goes to join JULES on her front porch. JULES tries to pass ALICE a beer. ALICE shakes her head.

JULES   Yeah. Smart. It's a new one they're rolling out and it is not good.

ALICE   What is it?

JULES   Coconut ale. Beer made from coconut. Like, I love coconuts as much as the next person but we might be wearing it out.

ALICE   We wore it out a long time ago.

JULES   How was the restaurant?

ALICE   Fine, I guess. Slow day today.

Moment. A comfortable silence.

ALICE   You smell.

JULES   What?

ALICE   You smell. It's not bad exactly. But it's not pleasant.

JULES   Thank you?

ALICE   Or is it the beer?

ALICE leans over to smell the beer. It's not the beer.

JULES   I went on a run. And haven't showered yet.

ALICE   Ah. You ever going back to work?

JULES   Every time with you. I work every day, Alice.

ALICE   I thought a little bit old banter would be nice. How's Yael?

JULES   She's at the university tonight for a symposium on Diasporic Art and Culture.

ALICE   You didn't want to go?

JULES   I love the idea of being with someone deeply entrenched in our culture but I can't listen to Black men talk about how they're the reason we have it.

ALICE God, there should be a city in Bronx Bay just for Black women. Wouldn't that be nice?

JULES Would the men need visas to visit? For booty calls.

ALICE Who needs sex when you're finally, actually free?

JULES Me. And you should too. It's part of the freedom.

ALICE Sex?

JULES Yes. Sexual freedom.

ALICE Meh.

Moment.

ALICE I'm sorry.

JULES Lorenzo finally convince you to apologize?

ALICE Sorta.
   He's a good man.

JULES He is.

ALICE I'm lucky he puts up with me. Although I guess at this point, I've got him trapped for the next eighteen years.

JULES He's not tra— Wait. What?

ALICE I'm pregnant.

JULES hugs ALICE.

JULES   Alice! That's amazing. How far along are you?

ALICE   Three months today. We're finally in the place where we can tell people.

JULES   Congratulations, Alice. Seriously.

ALICE   Thanks. After the last miscarriage, I wasn't sure if I still —
      Thanks.

JULES   Any names picked out yet?

ALICE   Lorenzo really likes Addison. I am not into it. My mom took me home for five days before she named me. I'd like to do something like that. Before that kind of thing would be illegal but luckily doctors here are more open to our cultural history.
      Anyway, you should get to know a child before you name them.

JULES   That's sweet.

ALICE   Yeah. I know we're not supposed to pre-gender our babies but I — I think it's a boy.

JULES   Yeah?

ALICE   Yeah. And that worries me.

JULES   Alice.

ALICE   I know we're safe here but for how long? If we start letting people in, how long before another black boy is murdered in the—

JULES   You don't have to do this with me.

ALICE   Jules, my brother was ripped out of his home

JULES   Alice, I was there.

ALICE   And they killed him. Shot him on the front lawn.

JULES   Alice, I don't want to re-live—

ALICE   And I know we're not supposed to talk about it.
But we need to talk about it.

JULES   Alice, we have talked about it.

ALICE   He loved you.

JULES   I loved him too. He's the reason I wanted to
move here and I—

ALICE   I miss him. And I just worry.

JULES   We moved here so we wouldn't need to worry
like this. Alice, we're safe. It's not—

ALICE   Safe for how long, Jules? You know how many
Black folk thought they were safe who are dead now?
Killed in their bedrooms, their living rooms, their cars—

JULES   Alice. You don't need to remind me about—

ALICE   I know it's not a perfect system but it falls
completely apart when we break the rules. At least I know,
in Bronx Bay, my son will not be targeted just for the color
of his skin. I need to know that it will stay that way.

JULES   Drew was the love of my life. We want the same
things.

ALICE   Do we?

Moment. It's heavy.

JULES   Alice, I'm so happy for you. You and Lorenzo
will make great parents.

ALICE   I'm not trying to be—

JULES   It's a nice night. Weather's nice. Sky is clear.

ALICE   Jules, I'm not—

JULES   I loved Drew. I still love Drew. I still have my
wedding dress hanging in the back of my closet. We've all
lost a lot to be here. And I haven't forgotten that.
     But I think strict definitions of blackness aren't any
better than anti-blackness.

ALICE   I'm not advocating for strict—

JULES   Yeah, you are. You haven't asked me about Yael.
You just made up your mind about her. And now you're
just moving forward regardless of the answer.

Moment.

ALICE   Good night Jules.

JULES   Night.

ALICE leaves the porch.

Scene 7

*It's a block party! LORENZO has a grill out on the front
lawn. ALICE is sitting on her porch, reading and watching*

LORENZO. JULES and YAEL are on their porch. Even though there are limited characters in the play and we only see a part of the block, it should be clear that this is an event. It's a cookout. It's a celebration.

YAEL   Y'all really do know how to turn up for a party.

JULES   All you gotta say is "cook out" and Lorenzo pulls out his grill and Alice puts on her playlist.

YAEL   This is celebrating the establishment of Bronx Bay right?

JULES   Yeah. And also just 'cause black folks love a cookout.

ALICE   *(from her porch)*
   Because we're the best at it.

LORENZO   I think other people just call this a barbecue.

ALICE   You mean white people.

They all start enjoying the music and their corner. Maybe a song comes on that they really like.

JULES   Are you really going to stay over there on your porch?

ALICE   Y'all can come over here.

JULES checks in with YAEL. They walk over.

JULES   Please tell me there is at least one SWV song on this playlist.

ALICE   There is not.

JULES   What?

ALICE   Leave the '90s behind Jules.

A moment. They keep dancing.
IZAAK enters with an object that is not a gun but the char-
acters recognize it as a gun and accept it as a gun. The more
out of place the "gun" is the better.
LORENZO sees him first.

LORENZO   Not now, Izaak.

IZAAK   Yael Gomez, you are under citizen's arrest.

JULES   The fuck?

IZAAK points the "gun" at YAEL.

JULES   You better put that down, Izaak.

IZAAK   I work for the citizen's police. Yael, you don't
belong here.

LORENZO   Lower the gun, Izaak.

IZAAK   Come peacefully and nothing needs to happen.

ALICE   What is going on?

IZAAK   Bronx Bay is Black only.
     Unless y'all don't stand for that anymore?

JULES   This is excessive.

IZAAK   How did you think it was regulated? You
thought, oh just because you love someone, it'll be fine?
You think you're the only person who's ever loved someone who wasn't the same race as you? You think you're
the only one who had to make a sacrifice? Yael, I won't
ask you again.

YAEL looks at JULES.

JULES   Wait, is this real?

YAEL   This feels extra as fuck.

JULES   Like how did we escalate so quickly to citizen's
arrest? That's what this is, right?

IZAAK   I'm just doing what the script tells me to do.

ALICE   It doesn't fit your character though.

IZAAK   Y'all couldn't say something about that while we
were in rehearsal? Does this feel like the right time?

LORENZO   So are we just done with this part?

JULES   This just doesn't feel right.

ALICE   This doesn't feel right.

IZAAK   This doesn't feel right.

LORENZO   This doesn't feel right.

YAEL   Let's start over.

Lights flash. END of Part 1.

Part 2

Prologue

JULES stands on stage in a colonial cos-play get up. She sits waiting and not patiently. YAEL comes out, dressed in all black, dressed up as a stereotypical film director from the 1940s.

YAEL   We're starting over.

JULES   I know that.

YAEL   I'm telling them.

JULES   You're not even in the right era.

YAEL   Are we even keeping this era this time?

JULES   Get off the stage!

YAEL takes her time getting off.

JULES   Alright. Damn. Please continue to take your time.
White folx call what I'm about to do "exposition." But the black folx in the audience know I'm about to preach. The world you're about to see ain't yours. It's not a parallel universe, it's not alternate reality. It's something else. It lives in the imagination of every person of color in this room.

When I get bored, I like to remove one historical event
and say to myself "would that make the playing field fair?"
What if there had been a revolt when Trump got elected?
Or, what if there had been no slavery? Like at all. Can you
even imagine the world without it? Our whole socio-eco-
system is built on the backs of people who look like me.
And I know, I know, I know. The playwright's hand is
showing. Get over it. That's kind of the point.

So, resetting the clock. Slavery never existed. And since
I know some of y'all are trifflin, let me be clear. The African diaspora due to the slavery of West Africans never
happened. The Roman still enslaved the Greeks and the
idea of slavery still exists but black people, my people,
were not slaves. We weren't forced onto ships, our names
and family histories weren't taken from us. That has been
erased.

During the Industrial Revolution, there was a great mi-
gration of Africans across the world but especially to Great
Britain and the colonies. Though no one came through
trying to steal resources from continental Africa, no one
came through with resources either.

The African people became incredibly advanced but the
only way to mass produce the technology was to take it
overseas themselves. Black folk all over the world came up
with brilliant inventions and became scientists, doctors,
inventors.

But thanks to general xenophobia, many of their inventions, the credit to who invented what, was stolen from
them. And when they tried to speak out against it, suddenly people started going missing. And then more and
more people went missing. Names vanished from history.

Y'all should know history is written by white folks
anyway.

JULES *leaves the stage.*

Scene 1

We're back on the block but in a different impossible time.
The houses have shifted.
LORENZO/IZAAK's house is JULES's house from Part 1.
ALICE/JULES's house is IZAAK's house from Part 1. YAEL's
house is in between the two.
ALICE is on the front porch cross-stitching. YAEL pulls up
with suitcases.

ALICE   You must be the new neighbor.

YAEL   I am.

ALICE   Well, welcome to the neighborhood.

YAEL   Thanks. Yael.

ALICE   Alice.

Moment.

YAEL   I was on the waitlist for a while. I didn't think I'd
be able to get in.

ALICE   Yeah, they're pretty strict about it. You'd think
you were asking to go to a different country and not just
a gated neighborhood.

YAEL   It's gorgeous here.

ALICE   It really is.

YAEL   How far along are you?

ALICE looks down.

ALICE   Oh. Is it that obvious?

YAEL   I'm sorry, I didn't mean to —

ALICE   No, it's okay. I guess it's safe to start telling
people. I just didn't realize I was showing. Three months.

YAEL   Oh wow. Congratulations.

ALICE   Thanks.

*JULES comes outside holding two lemonades. She kisses ALICE
quickly and then notices YAEL.*

JULES   Oh. Hi.

ALICE   New neighbor.

JULES   I'm Jules. Welcome to Bronx Bay.

YAEL   Thanks. I'm Yael.

JULES   Is it just you?

YAEL   Yeah.

JULES   Sorry, I didn't mean to pry.

YAEL   No, it's okay. I know mostly couples live on this
block.

JULES   Families, yeah.

YAEL   My partner broke up with me right before —
   Anyway, I had already put the down payment down so
here I am.

Moment.

ALICE   Would you want to come over for dinner?

YAEL   What?

ALICE   Dinner? I'm a chef. I'm cooking anyway for friends of ours. For Lorenzo and Izaak. It's Izaak's birthday and we always do a birthday dinner.

YAEL   I wouldn't want to— (intrude)

ALICE   I'm inviting you. It'd be nice to get to know our new neighbor.

YAEL   Um, yeah. Sure.

Moment.

ALICE   Oh no. Do you smell that?

ALICE *runs inside.*

JULES   She had something on the stove.

YAEL   I figured.

JULES   I'm sorry about your partner.

YAEL   Yeah, me too.

JULES   How long were you together?

YAEL   Ten years.

JULES   Shit.

YAEL   Yeah. Shit.
   Do you mind if I —

JULES   Oh, no. Sorry, I wasn't trying to keep you from moving in.

YAEL nods/smiles/something similar and then goes into her house. ALICE returns back out.

ALICE   Did she go inside?

JULES   She did.

ALICE   She's coming to dinner?

JULES   I think so.

ALICE   She knew I was pregnant.

JULES   Is it supposed to be a secret?

ALICE   You barely knew.

JULES   I did not barely know. It's not like I accidentally knocked you up.

ALICE   I think she's pregnant.

JULES   What?

ALICE   Pregnant women notice each other.

JULES   You think she's pregnant just because she could tell you were?

ALICE   Yes. I'm not showing yet.

JULES   Alice.

ALICE   What?
Can you imagine being a single mother? In a neighborhood like this?

JULES   Please don't be weird at dinner.

ALICE   I'm never —
I won't. But I know I'm right.

*JULES kisses ALICE and then goes inside. ALICE watches YAEL's
house.*

Scene 2

*At JULES/ALICE's house. ALICE puts the final plate on the table.
JULES opens a bottle of wine.*
  After a beat, LORENZO and IZAAK enter.

LORENZO   Are y'all clothed?

JULES   Oh my God.

*LORENZO and JULES hug while IZAAK and ALICE hug. And
then switch. JULES pours a glass of wine for everyone except
ALICE who drinks out of a juice box.*

IZAAK *(pointing to the juice box)*
  Why?

ALICE   I wanted to make you feel guilty that I can't
drink right now.

IZAAK   I don't ever feel guilty about drinking.

LORENZO   You should!

IZAAK   It's my birthday. You really gonna do me like
that on my birthday?

LORENZO kisses IZAAK playfully.

LORENZO   Happy birthday, babe.

JULES   What did y'all do today?

LORENZO   The same thing we do every year.

IZAAK   It's tradition.

LORENZO   Birthday sex in the morning, hiking in the—

ALICE   You really don't have to tell us you had birthday
sex.

LORENZO   Bitch, I just did.

JULES   And then hiking in the afternoon. How many
miles did you get?

ALICE   It's not weird for you to hear about your brother
having sex?

JULES   I'm an adult, Alice. God, I hope he's having sex.
And lots of it.

LORENZO   Thank you, baby sis.

JULES   You're welcome.

IZAAK   Only four miles this year.

JULES   Y'all getting out of shape?

ALICE   Oh!

Moment. They all turn to ALICE.

IZAAK   There are easier ways to demand attention.

ALICE   Before I forget again, I invited our new neighbor over.

JULES   You did what?

IZAAK   Who?

LORENZO   The woman that just moved in?

IZAAK   Why?

JULES   She's alone.

ALICE   And pregnant.

JULES   She's not pregnant.

LORENZO   But this block is supposed to be for families only and I didn't—

JULES   Her partner left her.

LORENZO   Oh. They still let her move in?

JULES   It's not a strict rule. The whole families thing. You two don't have kids yet.

LORENZO   Well, actually.

There's a knock on the front door.

ALICE   I'll get it.

ALICE leaves the room to get the door.

JULES   Well actually???

IZAAK   Not now.

LORENZO   I'll tell you later.

JULES   Did the adoption come through?

IZAAK   Not now!

ALICE returns with YAEL who is holding a casserole dish.

LORENZO   Oh. Let me take that.

JULES looks at LORENZO like "Why would you" and then takes it and sets it on the table.

LORENZO   Hi. I'm Lorenzo.

IZAAK   Izaak.

YAEL   Yael. Nice to meet you.

LORENZO   So you're our new neighbor?

YAEL   I am.

IZAAK   This neighborhood is perfect isn't it? Have you gotten a chance to stop by the school?

YAEL   Yeah. I did. It's great. I really like how they've updated the Montessori method to be more inclusive.

LORENZO   What do you do?

IZAAK   Lorenzo.

LORENZO   I'm not trying to be rude. I just—

YAEL   I'm a teacher. I actually will be working at the school in the fall.

ALICE   Oh, that's great! You can walk there. It's so close.

YAEL   Yeah.

An awkward silence.

ALICE   Are you pregnant?

YAEL   What?

ALICE   Are you pregnant?

JULES glares at ALICE. YAEL isn't sure how to answer. If it was awkward before, it just got more awkward.

LORENZO   We're adopting twins!

IZAAK   Lorenzo.

LORENZO   What? I wanted to make it less [awkward]. That's exciting, right?

JULES   THAT'S AMAZING.

JULES runs over to hug them both. ALICE keeps watching YAEL.

YAEL   Should I go?

JULES   Of course not. Alice is — She's hormonal.

IZAAK   That's not an excuse. Alice is just very intense in general.

YAEL   Congrats on twins.

IZAAK   Thank you. We just found out today.

ALICE   Let's cheers to it! Yael, wine? Unless you can't —

JULES   Alice.

ALICE   This is exciting!

YAEL   Wine would be great.

JULES nods and pours YAEL some wine. YAEL drinks it quickly. JULES pours her some more.

ALICE   Cheers!

They all raise their glasses and cheer.

JULES   Let's eat before the food gets cold.

They move toward the dinner table.

YAEL   How old will they be? The twins?

LORENZO   Five.

YAEL   Oh great. That's a great age.

IZAAK   We didn't want babies because everyone wants babies but teenagers seemed too —

YAEL   Five is perfect.

Scene 3

JULES comes out on stage. She's dressed like a talk-show host. IZAAK, LORENZO, and YAEL all come out as "contestants."

JULES   Welcome to DO YOU KNOW YOUR OWN HISTORY?

The sound of a recorded audience cheer.

JULES   Today we have three contestants but only one of them can be the winner. For $100, what is the Great Displacement?

IZAAK hits his buzzer first.

IZAAK   In 1850,[1] over a million black inventors and their families went missing. To this day, no one knows what happened.

JULES   Very good.

Recorded audience cheer.

JULES   Next question. For $500, what happened in 1965?[2]

IZAAK and YAEL both hit their buzzers.

---

1. For counter reference: The Compromise of 1850
2. For counter reference: The Voting Rights Act of 1965

JULES *(to* YAEL*)*
The system is showing me you were first.

YAEL   In the 1965, the Separatist Doctrine became law.
It ruled that any person of African descent who wanted to
"go back to Africa" would be given $1,000 and a plane
ticket so long as they signed the Separatist Visa vowing to
never return.

JULES   Excellent. You are correct.

Recorded audience cheer.

JULES   Now this one is tricky. For $1,000, what was the
Right to Birth Law of 1991?[3]

LORENZO hits his buzzer.

LORENZO   The Right to Birth Law of 1991 said that
any woman of color who had not married by age thirty
would agree to sterilization in order to help prevent overpopulation.

YAEL   Why was it just women of color?

JULES   I ask the questions. Good job.

Recorded audience cheer.

JULES   Next up. For $2,000, what was the—

YAEL   Wait. I thought it was all women. Why was it only
women of color?

---

3. For counter reference: The Civil Rights Act of 1991

JULES   Are you seriously going to stop the game for this?

YAEL   Yes. I want to know why.

IZAAK   Because in the '90s women of color were believed to be more fertile than white women.

YAEL   Doesn't this law still exist?

JULES   NEXT QUESTION. For $2,000, what was the Great Revolution of 2007?

Lights change.

Scene 4

At night, JULES is on her front porch, writing in a notebook. She's spacing out every now and again. YAEL comes out on her front porch to smoke cigarette. Before she can light it —

JULES   Those are illegal here.

YAEL   What?

JULES   Cigarettes.

YAEL   Here as in the neighborhood?

JULES   Yeah.

YAEL   Oh.

YAEL throws the unlit cigarette into a plant.

JULES   I used to drive about twenty miles north just so I could smoke one.

YAEL   Is it because of the kids? Second-hand?

JULES   Yeah. Probably. To some extent anyway. I think
to some extent, people just like controlling other people.

YAEL   May I come over there?

JULES   Of course.

YAEL *leaves her porch to join* JULES.

JULES   I'm sorry about Alice earlier.

YAEL   It's fine. This neighborhood is supposed to be for
families so I get that she's just a bit intense.

JULES   Intense is an understatement.

YAEL   My parents are like that. My dad is super, hyper-
intense and my mom is the chill, anything-goes one.

JULES   Does that make me your mom?

YAEL   Oh, that's weird.

JULES   Why is that weird?

Moment.

JULES   I do think some of it is pregnancy brain. Like it
just kind of makes you loopy.

YAEL   Yeah. I know.

JULES   Oh.

YAEL   I mean I figured. Wait. Shit, I —
    I was pregnant. Before.

JULES   Oh.

YAEL   Yeah. When we applied to move into this neighborhood, I was pregnant.

JULES   Oh my God. I'm so sorry about Alice.

YAEL   No, it's —
    It's okay.

JULES   It definitely, definitely isn't.

YAEL   Yeah.

JULES   You can have that cigarette if you want it.

YAEL laughs or something similar.

YAEL   I'm okay.

JULES   Probably for the best. The neighbors across the
street are the worst.

Moment.

JULES   What happened? Can I ask that?

YAEL   You can ask.
    Um, I miscarried.

JULES   I'm sorry.

YAEL   Yeah. My third one.

JULES   Oh shit.

YAEL   Yeah.

JULES   After three miscarriages, don't they sterilize —

YAEL   Yeah.

A hard moment.

JULES   I didn't get married by thirty, so same thing happened to me. Different reason obviously. There's a reason Alice is pregnant and not me.

YAEL   I'm sorry.

JULES shrugs.

JULES   We signed a deal with the devil, you know? Overpopulation was a major —
      We did what we had to.

YAEL   Feels like eugenics. Like a new sneaky way to police our bodies.

JULES   Yeah. It's maybe a little bit of that too.

Moment

YAEL   Was Alice married before —

JULES   She was. Hilarious. I met her when she was married. To a guy named Andy.

YAEL   Oh.

JULES   Yeah. I'm not saying bisexuality doesn't exist. It does. I am bisexual. But Alice? Alice! Alice is the gayest person I've ever met.

YAEL   Was she cross-stitching a cat when I got in?

JULES   Yes! Gay. Gay as fuck.

YAEL   Why did she —

JULES   She wasn't sure she'd find the one before she was thirty so she married a man so she could stay . . . you know, not sterilized.

YAEL   Fuck.

JULES   Yeah.

YAEL   I wonder how they came up with the age thirty.

JULES   Men seem to think women expire after our twenties.

YAEL   Yeah. They said they were doing it to prevent "geriatric pregnancies," like that was supposed to be make me feel better.
    I think I could've been a good mom.

JULES   You still can be. Adoption.

YAEL   You have to be married to adopt.

JULES   Get married.

YAEL   It's not that easy.

JULES   Someone as attractive as you. You could get married tomorrow.

Moment.

YAEL   I should head home.

JULES   Okay. Good night.

YAEL   Good night.

YAEL heads back to her house but lingers on her porch. JULES writes in her notebook. They look at each other. The moment is a little tense. YAEL goes inside. JULES goes back to writing.

Scene 5

The set shifts to show an old-school swing dance party. JULES comes out in a hoop skirt and IZAAK comes out in a suit.
      Though they swing dance as they talk, the music doesn't match the dance. It'd be fun if it was Too Short or LL Cool J. Something upbeat.

JULES   If this was *Color Struck,* you and I would tear up the dance floor.

IZAAK   I always tear up the dance floor.

JULES   I, of course, would have a mental crisis about my complexion.

IZAAK   I would leave for another woman.

JULES   We'd both romanticize the south.

IZAAK   Colorism has changed a lot since then.

JULES   The tragic mulatto.

IZAAK   The legacy of minstrelsy was hard to shake off.

Moment. The song changes to soul music. They continue to dance together.

IZAAK   If this was *Dutchman*, I would end up dead.

JULES   Black folk always end up in dead. Even in our own plays.

IZAAK   Does that make you Lula?

JULES   If this was *Dutchman*, I wouldn't be in it. Black women didn't exist in plays yet, I guess.

Moment. The song changes to ragtime. They continue to dance together.

IZAAK   Well, I'm not a colored girl and I've for sure never considered suicide.

JULES   Lucky you.

IZAAK   Didn't need to. The cops will come for me first.

Music changes to jazz. They stop dancing.

JULES   When do we get to be happy?

IZAAK   You're not happy?

JULES   I mean here. In this space. On this stage.
    Were we ever happy?
    Are we allowed to be happy onstage?

IZAAK   In *colored girls,* they were happy.

JULES   They were also abused.

IZAAK   What about *Rachel?*

JULES   The lynching play?

IZAAK   Oh yeah. You right.

They both think for a moment.

IZAAK   Sometimes being black is tragic.

JULES   Sometimes it's lit though.

IZAAK   Happiness isn't dramatically compelling. There's no conflict in joy.

JULES   I don't think that's true.

Music changes to R&B. JULES, by herself, waltzes offstage. IZAAK pulls out a mic as if he's about sing. Lights change.

Scene 6

The next day, on LORENZO and IZAAK's front porch, JULES and LORENZO sit drinking beer and playing cards.

LORENZO   There is no way she'd go for it.

JULES   Why not?

LORENZO   You think Alice, Alice who is absolutely the most dramatic human either of us have ever met, will be okay with you taking a second wife?

JULES   Yes. Because it's a sham marriage.

LORENZO   Is it?

JULES   Yael can stay in this neighborhood . . . what?
Tops a year before someone starts freaking out about her
not having kids? And she wants kids. How dumb is it that
the only reason she can't have a kid is because she's un-
married?

LORENZO   Jules. There is no world in which Alice is
okay with this.

JULES   It'll be just a fast ceremony. Isn't wild that
polygamy is legal but single-parent adoption isn't? Like,
who woulda thought that I, a woman, could have two
wives but my neighbor, a single woman —

LORENZO   Your neighbor who is hot

JULES   What?

LORENZO   Come on. Jules. Do you think I'm blind?

JULES   I think you're gay.

LORENZO   And what? Heternormative beauty standards
weren't still pushed on me our whole childhood? I can
think a woman is hot.

JULES   I think gay men see attractiveness differently.

LORENZO   You're not attracted to her?

JULES   That's not why I want to do it.

LORENZO   Sure.

LORENZO plays a card.

JULES   Did you just win?

LORENZO   I did. Play again?

JULES nods. LORENZO shuffles the cards.

JULES   I think every woman that wants a child should have one.

LORENZO   You're projecting now.

JULES   I just —
  I'm going to ask her.

LORENZO   You're going to ask Yael to marry you? Or you're going to ask Alice's permission?

JULES   Yes. To both.

LORENZO deals out the cards.

LORENZO   Jules, honey, no.

JULES   What?

LORENZO   You cannot ask your wife if you can have another wife.

JULES   There are tons of people with two partners.

LORENZO   And you are not one of those people. Well, hold on. Alice, your pregnant wife, is not one of those people.

They start to play. (This is more fun if it's a game we don't recognize. A new made-up game to match the "made-up" history of the play.)

JULES   Okay, who has a bigger heart than Alice?

LORENZO   Jules.

JULES   If Izaak came home one day and met someone who he felt . . . connected to and wanted to help, wouldn't you want to help too?

LORENZO   Connected to?

JULES   You know, like No, not like —
    She came out on the porch last night.

LORENZO   Jules.

JULES   Nothing happened. It was just —
    The sadness in her eyes, Lorenzo. It was like I have to help her.

Moment.

LORENZO   Are you excited about the baby?

JULES   What baby?

LORENZO   Jules!

JULES   Oh! Alice? Yes, of course I am. You randomly changed the subject. How I was supposed to —

LORENZO   I was trying to remind you what you're sacrificing.

JULES   I'm not sacrificing anything. I'm trying to—

LORENZO   I think you're looking for a reason to cheat.
Again.
      Alice, your wife, is pregnant, Jules. You need to commit
to that. Stop looking for—

JULES   I could commit to both of them.

LORENZO   You don't even know Yael.

JULES   You wouldn't get this, Lorenzo. No one cut you
up like a science experiment and told you to deal with it.

LORENZO   Jules.

JULES   I'm done talking about this.

They continue to play in silence.

Scene 7

*ALICE comes out as a famous actress dressed up on Oscar
Night about to receive an award. She walks toward the
podium. Audience applause.*

ALICE   What an honor. You know, when they told me I
was receiving this award, I just started crying. Like ugly
crying. I thought, "Who, me?" I am just so honored—

JULES comes out dressed the same as ALICE.

JULES   This is my bit. You had Part 1, remember?

ALICE   Oh. Sorry.

ALICE leaves the stage.

JULES   What an honor. You know, when they told me I
was receiving this award, I just started crying, Like ugly
crying. I thought —
     You know what? Actually, no. I didn't cry. I'm not
honored. Why did this take so long? How much longer
did you think you could keep ignoring black excellence?
Why did I need to have my own studio lot, star in movies
I produced, and work my ass twice as hard as everyone else
to stand up here in front you and tell you how honored I
am? Fuck that.
     This should've been mine years ago. You should've said
something years ago. You can't expect me, expect any of
us to fall over and bow when you finally take the time to
notice we've been here this whole time. Take your awards.
I don't want it. Because I deserved it years ago and it's not
on me that you didn't realize it until now.

JULES leaves the stage.

Scene 8

*ALICE and YAEL sit awkwardly in the living room of ALICE/
JULES's house. A moment.*

ALICE   Jules said she'd be here soon.

YAEL   Cool.

ALICE   I, um
     Do you know what this is about?

YAEL   She said she had to ask me something. I —
     When I knocked, I expected her to answer. I didn't, I
didn't know you'd be home.

ALICE   Yeah. Right.

YAEL   She didn't say anything to you?

ALICE   She said she had something to ask me. I'm sorry
I was so —
    I didn't realize you had —

YAEL   It's okay. I'm not even sure why I told Jules.

ALICE   She has one of those personalities. People are
always just telling her things. It's actually—

JULES comes running in.

JULES   I'm sorry I was late. I got caught up at work.

ALICE   Jules, what's going on?

JULES   I have something very important to ask both
of you.

Moment.

ALICE   And that is?

JULES   Marry me.

ALICE   We're already married.

YAEL   I don't —

JULES   Okay, so I thought about it and I thought about
it a lot, Yael, you want kids, right?

YAEL   I . . . what?

ALICE   Jules!

JULES   So marry me.

ALICE   What the fuck is going on?

JULES   And then we can connect our homes and like raise our kids together.

ALICE   Have you lost your mind?

JULES   Alice, I wanted you to be here so you could see it's not romantic. It's —

ALICE   It's absolutely batshit.

IZAAK comes out.

IZAAK   Okay, okay, okay. Wait a minute.

JULES   You're not in this scene.

IZAAK   I'm aware. I'm barely in any scene.

IZAAK walks over to an audience member.

IZAAK   *(meaning the program)*
   Can I see that?

If the audience member gives IZAAK the program, great! If not, IZAAK goes to get a program from a house manager or an usher.

IZAAK   Thank you.

IZAAK opens the program.

IZAAK   What exactly is this play?

JULES   It's a play about blackness.

IZAAK   Sure, sure. Is the playwright black?

YAEL   Of course she is.

IZAAK   I mean, it says Afro-Latine, so again, my question stands.

JULES   She's Black, Izaak.

LORENZO comes out.

IZAAK   Okay. And she's from Arkansas?

LORENZO   L.A. She grew up in L.A.

JULES   Neither of you are in this scene.

IZAAK   So how is a sorta Black girl from L.A. gonna write a play about blackness?

LORENZO   That's not even the worst part. She grew up in Malibu.

JULES   She didn't grow up in Malibu.

LORENZO   I saw online, in an interview, her dad had a house there.

JULES   That's not where she grew up.

IZAAK   Cool. So a rich black girl from maybe not Malibu—

YAEL   She isn't rich. She grew up poor!

IZAAK   In Malibu?

ALICE   So are we just done with the play then? I got people I wanna see.

IZAAK   I'm just saying. What makes her the authority on blackness? What is this play even about anyway?

YAEL   Fair. Part 1 felt like —

LORENZO   Like it was about to be torture porn.

YAEL   Right. And so far Part 2 is some sort of comedy of errors about Black maternity? But with queer people.

IZAAK   So people came out to see this and are gonna go home and say this is what blackness is. This is what queerness is.
And we're all okay with that?

Moment.

JULES   I mean, technically she's writing our lines. Still. So I don't know that we can be not okay with it.

IZAAK   I'm just tired of this, you know? Blackness isn't a monolith. So how do you write a play about it and then ask Black bodies to get on stage and just do it and just let your version be the version? How is that okay?

ALICE   That's part of the gig though, isn't it? I mean, that's how it works. We get on stage, say some lines, go home. It's how it works.

IZAAK   And maybe something's broken there. Blackness is not a monolith. There is not a singular experience.

ALICE   It's not like she's the only Black playwright.
There are other voices.

JULES   Right. So can we finish the play, please? You can
go see a Branden Jacobs-Jenkins play after this one and,
boom. Problem solved.

IZAAK   No. Problem not solved.

YAEL   Okay. On the real, are you just mad you didn't
have a lot of lines?

IZAAK   I'm mad that I have to put on all these masks
and none of them seem to fit right.

Moment. JULES's phone vibrates.

JULES   Oh.

IZAAK   Oh?

JULES   What does blackness mean to you?

YAEL   What?

JULES   She just texted. The playwright. She's asking us.

ALICE   And we're supposed to just answer.

JULES   Yeah.

*Moment. The moment can take as long as it needs to. Each
actor answers the question and says what blackness means
to them. It can be as poetic or as plain as they want. This
moment should feel honest. It's the most important part of
the play.*

After they're done, "Blackness is not a monolith" should be projected if possible. *If not, a creative way to display it (for example, there are five words in "Blackness is not a monolith," and maybe the actors all hold up a poster with each word).*

"Blackness is not a monolith. END OF PLAY.*"*

END OF PLAY.